DISASTER ALERT!

Ocean Storm Alert!

Carrie Gleason

Crabtree Publishing Company
www.crabtreebooks.com

presented by:

Crabtree Publishing Company

www.crabtreebooks.com

To Charlotte and summer camp

Coordinating editor: Ellen Rodger

Project editor: Rachel Eagen

Copy editor: Adrianna Morganelli

Indexer: Adrianna Morganelli

Book design and production coordinator: Rosie Gowsell

Cover design: Rob MacGregor

Photo research: Allison Napier

Consultant: Martin Lisius, Prairie Pictures

Photographs: Brian and Cherry Alexander/ Photo Researchers, Inc: p.18; AP/ Wide World Photos: p. 17 (top), p. 19 (bottom), p. 21, p. 24, p. 25, p. 27, p. 28, p. 29; Tony Aruza/ CORBIS/ MAGMA: p. 17 (bottom); Bettman/ CORBIS/ MAGMA: p. 5 (bottom), p. 20; Peter Bowater/ Photo Researchers, Inc: p. 3, p. 5 (top); Brand X Pictures/ Getty Images: p. 19 (top), p. 26; Lynette Cook/ SCIENCE PHOTO LIBRARY: p. 15; Ewing Galloway/ Index Stock Imagery: p. 1; S.P. Gillette/ CORBIS: p. 12; Jeffery Greenberg/ Photo Researchers, Inc: p. 27 (right); Paolo Koch/ Photo Researchers, Inc: p. 13 (bottom); John Lund/ Getty Images: p. 4; Andrew Martinez/ Photo Researchers, Inc: p.6 (all); National Oceanic and Atmospheric Administration/ Department of Commerce: p.22 (top), p.23 (top); Francoise Sauze/ Photo Researchers, Inc: p. 15; Ray Soto/ CORBIS: p. 13 (top)

Illustrations: Dan Pressman: p. 6, p. 7, p. 12, p. 14, p. 16; David Wysotski, Allure Illustrations: pp. 30-31

Maps: Jim Chernishenko: p. 9, pp. 10-11

Cover: Boats start to list, or turn on their side, in the face of high waves.

Contents: Rotating lenses and a motor cause the light from a lighthouse to scan the water. The light helps guide boats to shore.

Title page: A boat battles overpowering waves in an ocean storm.

Crabtree Publishing Company

www.crabtreebooks.com   1-800-387-7650

Printed in Canada/062016/TT20160525

Library of Congress Cataloging-in-Publication data

Gleason, Carrie, 1973-
    Ocean storm alert! / written by Carrie Gleason.
        p. cm. -- (Disaster alert!)
    Includes index.
    ISBN 0-7787-1579-5 (rlb)-- ISBN 0-7787-1611-2 (pbk)
    1. Tsunamis--Juvenile literature. 2. Whirlpools--Juvenile literature. 3. Cyclones--Juvenile literature. 4. Storms--Juvenile literature. I. Title. II. Series.
    GC221.5.G54 2005
    551.46--dc22
                                            2004013055
                                            LC

Published in Canada
Crabtree Publishing
616 Welland Ave.
St. Catharines, Ontario
L2M 5V6

Published in the United States
Crabtree Publishing
PMB 59051
350 Fifth Avenue, 59th Floor
New York, New York 10118

Published in the United Kingdom
Crabtree Publishing
Maritime House
Basin Road North, Hove
BN41 1WR

Published in Australia
Crabtree Publishing
3 Charles Street
Coburg North
VIC, 3058

Table of Contents

Tempest-Tossed

Since ancient times, sailors have tried to predict the weather when at sea. Before modern satellite and other forecasting tools, sailors depended on signs from the sky, the wind, and the sea to predict the weather. If the sky looked red at dawn, it meant that rain and storms were on the way. If the sky was red at sunset, it meant the next day's weather would be fine.

Many sailors have been caught in rough seas during severe tropical storms and hurricanes. Sailors have run into unavoidable dangers such as thick fog, icebergs, or whirlpools. Some sailors have survived, and lived to tell the tale, while others have met their end in the deep waters of the world's oceans. Today, the ocean floors are littered with countless shipwrecks.

Lighthouses help people guide their boats safely to shore.

What is a disaster?
A disaster is a destructive event that affects the natural world and human communities. Some disasters are predictable and others occur without warning. Coping successfully with a disaster depends on a community's preparation.

According to an old sailors' tale, a red sky in the morning means that sailors will have rough seas.

On shore and at sea

Ocean storms not only affect ships at sea. Storms also wreak havoc when they hit shore, by destroying workplaces, roads, and other **infrastructure**. Crowded cities and villages stand on coastlines all over the world, in the path of destructive storms. People continue to risk the dangers of the sea to travel, transport goods, catch fish, and drill for oil. The oceans are an invaluable resource, since they provide us with food, recreational activities, and transportation routes, but they can also be the cause of devastating natural disasters.

Poseidon's revenge

The ancient Greeks believed that powerful gods controlled different parts of nature. The god of the sea was called Poseidon. According to a Greek myth, Poseidon became angry with a war hero, named Odysseus, who killed the god's son. In revenge for the deed, Poseidon used his three-pronged spear, called a trident, to whip up fierce ocean storms that prevented Odysseus' ship from returning home for ten years!

Wild, Wet, and Windy

Ocean waters are mighty, powerful forces that are always moving. Even on days that the surface of the ocean appears calm, there are strong ocean currents, sometimes called "rivers of the ocean," that move water around the world. There are three main forces that keep ocean waters moving: sunlight, winds, and the rotation of the Earth.

Sunlight

Energy from the sun moves ocean waters all around the world. The sun gives off powerful rays of **heat energy** that warm the surface of the oceans. The tropics receive the most heat because they are closest to the equator, which is the invisible line that runs around the center of the Earth. The polar regions, the Arctic and Antarctica, receive the least amount of heat energy.

Storm cycle

1. The sun heats the water until it turns into a gas and rises into the air, or evaporates. Cooler air rushes in to replace the rising air, which creates high winds.

2. Water vapor condenses into storm clouds.

3. Precipitation falls when the clouds become heavy with water. The storm builds as more hot air is sucked into the clouds.

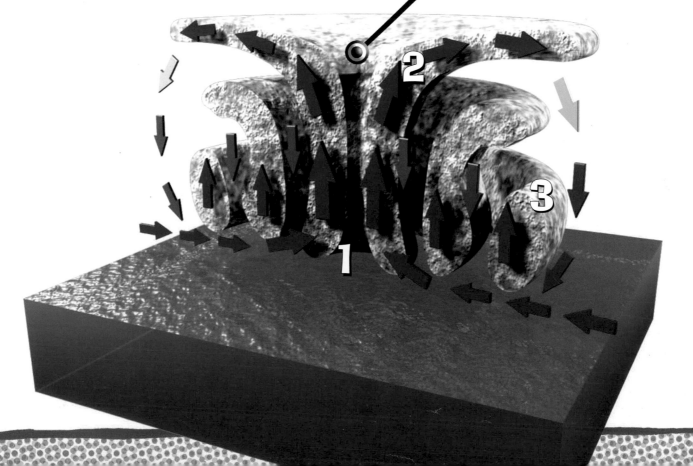

Wind and air pressure

Air moves in a continuous cycle around the Earth with help from the sun. The sun's heat creates areas of high and low air pressure. Air moves from an area of high pressure to an area of low pressure. Cold air from the North and South Poles creates high pressure, while warm air around the equator creates low pressure. As warm air rises, cold air, or high pressure, rushes in from the poles to replace it.

Naming the winds

Warm air moves north and south from either side of the equator, where it gradually cools and sinks. As the air begins to sink, it splits. Some of the air moves back toward the equator, while the rest of it continues on toward the poles. Trade winds are the winds that rush back toward the equator. Winds that continue on toward the poles are called westerly winds. Polar, or easterly, winds reach the poles, where they cool down. The three main wind systems, the trades, westerlies, and easterlies, occur in both hemispheres and are known as prevailing winds.

Earth spins on its axis in an east to west direction. This spinning helps create the three prevailing wind systems.

1. Easterlies

2. Westerlies

3. Trade Winds

The Coriolis Effect

The Coriolis Effect is the name given to the impact that the Earth's rotation, or spinning, has on wind and ocean currents. In the Northern Hemisphere, winds deflect to the right of their original course. In the Southern Hemisphere, they deflect to the left.

Ocean currents also curve because of the Coriolis Effect. In the Northern Hemisphere, ocean waters circulate in clockwise gyres, or giant circular currents of surface waters. In the Southern Hemisphere, currents circulate in counterclockwise gyres.

Tide is in

In the Bay of Fundy, between the Canadian provinces of New Brunswick and Nova Scotia, high tide raises the water level by 50 feet (15 meters). Tides can also move extremely fast, traveling as much as ten miles per hour (sixteen km/h). The rush of the incoming tide easily sweeps people and small animals off their feet, and into the water.

Tide is out

During low tide, rocks, reefs, and sand dunes on the ocean floor are exposed, which can cause a ship to "run aground" or hit the bottom. This can tear holes in the ship's hull, or body. Sailors can find themselves stranded until the water level rises enough to set sail once again. At low tide, some people go digging for clams and other marine life that live in the mud.

Tides

Twice a day, water levels rise and fall along the Earth's ocean coastlines in cycles called tides. When the water level is high, the tide is said to be high, or in. When the water level is low, the tide is said to be low, or out. Tides are caused by the pull of the Moon's gravity on Earth. Gravity is the force of attraction that surrounds bodies in the universe. The gravitational pull of the Moon is especially strong when the Moon is directly overhead. This causes water to bulge toward the Moon, resulting in high tide. In most places, there are two high tides each day, one as the Moon is overhead, and a second as the Moon is overhead on the opposite side of the earth.

Waves

Ocean waves form by wind blowing across the water's surface. As the wind blows, energy is transferred to the water, creating a wave. A wave looks like water being pushed along the surface of the ocean, but it is actually energy moving from water particle to water particle. The size of the wave depends on how fast the wind is blowing, how long the wind has been blowing in the same direction, and the fetch, or area of open water that is being affected by the wind. The greater all of these factors, the bigger the wave.

Prevailing winds blowing hard and continuously over the oceans create the biggest waves. Waves are measured from the crest, or top, to the trough, or bottom. The average height of an ocean wave is about twelve feet (four meters). During a storm, waves may grow to over 33 feet (10 meters).

Ocean currents

Ocean currents are large bodies of warm or cold water that move around the oceans. Currents are the result of winds blowing over the surface of the ocean, as well as **convection** below the water's surface. Convection occurs when cold water warms up and rises to the surface. It occurs at a depth of water known as the thermocline.

The prevailing winds create three major current systems in each hemisphere. They are the equatorial current system, the subtropical gyre, and the subpolar gyre.

Deeper down, cold ocean currents are created by differences in water **density**, which are caused by temperature and **salinity**. Cold, salty water is more dense than warm, fresh water, so it sinks. Sinking water is replaced by water that is less dense. This process sets deep currents in motion.

The major ocean currents of the world circulate either clockwise or counterclockwise.

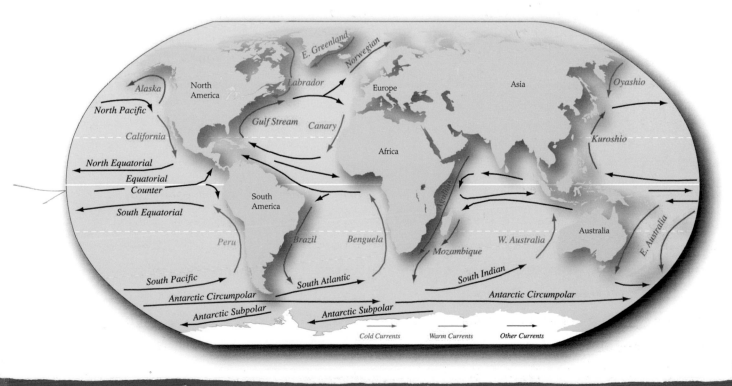

Path of a Storm

Different parts of the world are affected by different kinds of ocean storms and sea dangers. In the tropics, or warm areas near the equator, tropical storms and hurricanes toss ships about on huge waves before moving inland to cause damage, such as floods, to coastal areas. In polar regions, icebergs, ice floes, and ice packs tear holes in boats or crush them like tin cans.

Ocean currents, air pressure, and heat from the sun all cause the oceans to behave in particular ways. Some parts of the world are vulnerable to several kinds of ocean dangers, while others are safer from weather and other ocean hazards.

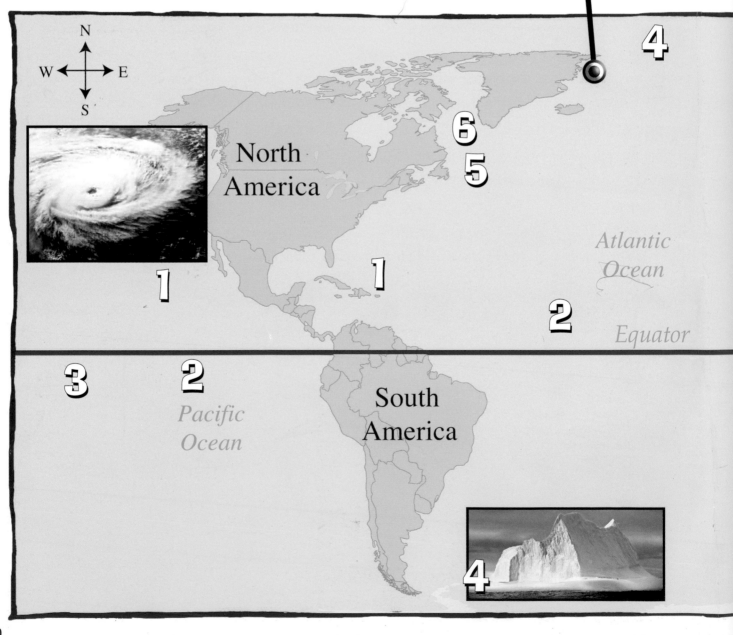

1. Hurricanes

Hurricanes occur in the Atlantic and eastern Pacific. The storms are called cyclones in the Indian Ocean, and typhoons in the western Pacific.

2. Tropical Storms

Tropical storms are weaker than hurricanes and occur in the warm equatorial regions.

3. Tsunamis

Tsunamis form along the "Ring of Fire," an area of active undersea volcanoes and earthquakes in the Pacific Ocean.

4. Icebergs

Icebergs break free from glaciers in the Arctic and Antarctica.

5. Whirlpools

Whirlpools are found off the coast of Norway and off the coast of Japan.

6. Fog

The East Coast of Canada experiences an average of 120 days of fog per year.

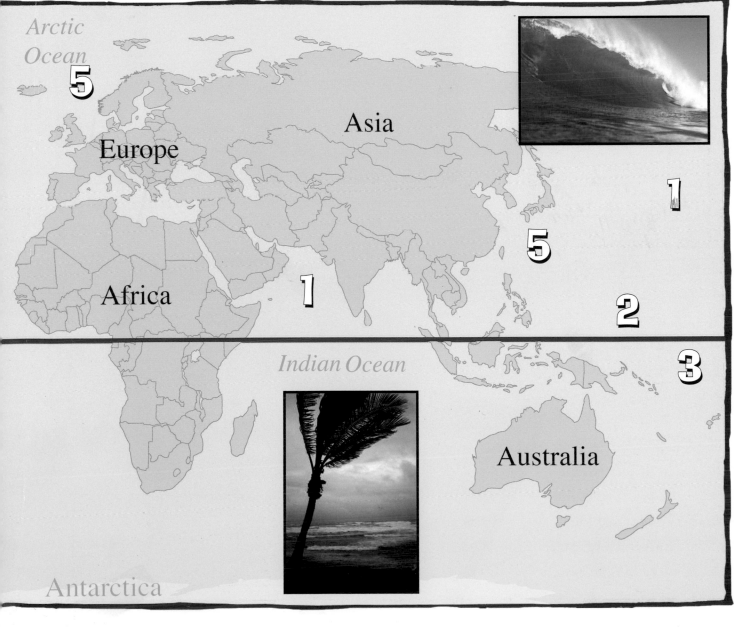

Turbulent Tropics

Hurricanes are the fiercest and most powerful storms on Earth. They occur in the tropics, which receive the greatest amount of heat from the sun. In the Indian Ocean, these storms are called cyclones, while they are known as typhoons in the western Pacific Ocean.

Hurricanes

Hurricanes form in the tropics during the summer and early fall. Surface water temperatures must be at least 80° Fahrenheit (27° Celsius) for a hurricane to form. The air over the sea becomes hot and moist, then rises and cools to form clouds. Cooler air rushes in to replace the hot rising air, which creates winds up to 74 miles per hour (120 km/h). Clouds gather masses of water and dump it as torrential rain. As hurricanes move toward land and further away from the tropics, they lose power as they lose heat. Hurricanes can last about nine days and travel as far as 3,000 miles (5,000 km). Tropical storms are slightly weaker, with winds up to 73 miles per hour (118 km/h).

It is possible for sailors to brave a hurricane at sea, but it is very risky. Most sailors try to avoid these storms.

The low pressure area in the center of a hurricane is called the eye. The eye is about 12 miles (20 km) wide. The hurricane itself can be up to 500 miles (800 km) wide.

Waterspouts look like tornadoes over water.

Waterspouts

Waterspouts form on the edge of hurricanes when moist, warm air is pulled into a rotating column of upward-moving air over the water. Winds in a waterspout rotate at 40 miles per hour (64 km/h). Waterspouts can cause sailboats to tip over.

Monsoons

Monsoons are seasonal winds that blow continuously over India and Asia. Wet monsoons bring heavy rainfall to India from June to October, often causing floods. Rainstorms are brought in by cool, moist sea winds that blow in from the Indian Ocean. The strong monsoon winds change direction in the winter, so that the cool, continental air rushes out to sea. This is called the dry monsoon. For many centuries, trading ships have depended on monsoon winds to carry their boats back and forth across the Indian Ocean.

Sailing through the storm

Sailors caught in a hurricane at sea first see thick, black clouds, then heavy rains start to fall as high winds kick up. Huge waves break over the ship and toss it about for hours. Then, the ship enters the eye of the hurricane, where the skies are clear and blue. A little while later, the sky darkens again and the winds begin to roar. After several hours, the air grows still and the clouds break up as the ship sails out of the storm.

Storm surge

Hurricanes can cause water to pile up in waves known as storm surges. In open water, the waves spread back out, but closer to land, the shallow ocean floor causes the waves to build up high. Storm surges cause terrible floods that damage waterfronts.

Monster Waves

Some ocean dangers come from the sea itself, and have very little to do with the weather. Strong ocean currents can damage deep sea oil rigs. Other dangers include tsunamis, rogue waves, and whirlpools.

Tsunamis

Tsunamis are caused by underwater earthquakes and volcanic eruptions, and they are the largest waves of all. Earthquakes occur when two **tectonic plates** collide or slide past each other. When an earthquake occurs under the ocean, the ocean bottom shakes. This movement causes the water above to become **displaced**. Waves of energy spread out in all directions from the source of the vibrations in ever-widening circles. As the tsunami approaches shore, the waves rub against the sea floor. **Friction** causes the waves to slow down and build from behind, creating huge piles of water that crash onto the shore.

Rogue waves

Sometimes, groups of large ocean waves caused by a storm slam into a powerful ocean current passing in the opposite direction. When this happens, several storm waves pile up to form gigantic waves called rogue or freak waves. These waves can be more than 100 feet (30 meters) tall and can bury cargo ships beneath the sea. Rogue waves are most common off the coasts of Japan, Florida, and Alaska. Currently, a project known as WaveAtlas monitors the oceans with satellites. Over the next few years, oceanographers hope to analyze these satellite images to help them better understand why freak waves occur.

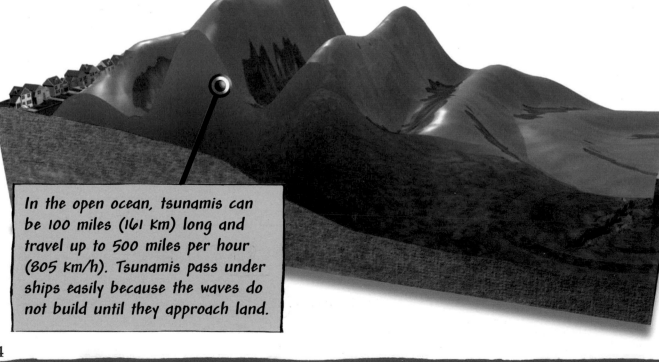

In the open ocean, tsunamis can be 100 miles (161 km) long and travel up to 500 miles per hour (805 km/h). Tsunamis pass under ships easily because the waves do not build until they approach land.

Whirlpools

Whirlpools are revolving currents formed by the meeting of opposite-moving ocean currents, the collision between currents and tides, or tides moving along uneven coasts. When churning, whirlpools make a loud sucking noise. Small ships may become trapped and wrecked by the force of the revolving water. Larger ships find steering difficult. The best-known whirlpool is the Maelstrom, off the coast of Norway. Here, currents flowing through **fjords** and around islands create the whirlpool. Another well-known whirlpool is named the Old Sow and is formed between New Brunswick and Maine.

Physical barriers in the water can create whirlpools because they disrupt the regular flow of water.

Krakatoa

On August 27, 1883, an undersea volcano called Krakatoa erupted in the Indian Ocean. The force of the explosion caused a tsunami with waves more than twelve stories high. The waves were so powerful that small islands were washed away and thousands of boats were sunk. As the waves circled the southern tip of Africa, they entered the Atlantic Ocean, traveling at 400 miles per hour (640 km/h). The tsunami destroyed more than 300 communities and killed over 36,000 people.

Scientists believe that the waves from Krakatoa circled the globe two or three times before running out of energy.

El Niño and La Niña

Normally, trade winds blow east to west across the Pacific Ocean, carrying the top layer of warm water away from the continent of South America, westward to Australia and Indonesia. As a result, places in the western Pacific have a wetter climate. About every seven years, an unusually warm ocean current travels eastward to South America. This warm current is called El Niño.

El Niño

El Niño usually arrives in South America in December, bringing warm waters and rain to the coasts. El Niño can last anywhere from three to eighteen months. During that time, the effects it has on world **climate** can be catastrophic.

El Niño and world weather

In an El Niño year, the trade winds change direction, carrying warm water toward South America rather than away from the continent. Indonesia and Australia suffer from droughts and forest fires instead of receiving rain. Meanwhile, countries along the coast of South America, such as Peru and Ecuador, receive much more rain that usual, which causes floods.

The effects of El Niño are also felt in North America. Heavier rainfall comes to the southeastern coast of the United States. Milder winters occur in Alaska and western Canada, while the southeastern United States is colder than usual. Many of these changes in North American weather occur because El Niño affects the jet stream, a high altitude, fast moving air current that moves weather across the continent.

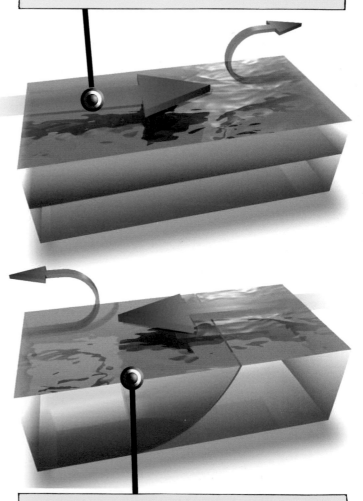

During an El Niño year, the trade winds falter and bring unusually warm water to South America.

During a normal year, the trade winds blow warm waters toward Australia and Indonesia.

El Niño and wildlife

Cold water carries **nutrients** that are the basis of the ocean food chain. As cold waters are warmed by the sun, **plankton** grow. Plankton are tiny organisms that feed the smaller fish in the oceans, which are food for larger fish. In a normal year, fishers off the coasts of South America catch a huge amount of fish and other marine life in these cold waters. During an El Niño year, the warm ocean current prevents the nutrient–rich cold water from reaching the surface and the food chain is broken.

La Niña

La Niña is a cold water event that happens about every four years. During La Niña, surface temperatures in the Pacific are colder than usual by about 1° Fahrenheit (0.5° C) for approximately six months. The trade winds that blow east to west across the Pacific are stronger and drive the warm water current further west. During La Niña, some scientists have noted an increased number of hurricanes in the Atlantic, while monsoons in Asia are wetter than usual.

(above) El Niño is Spanish for Christ Child. Peruvian fishers named it because it happens in December, when the Christ Child was born.

(top) In an El Niño year, prevailing winds that normally blow toward Africa move south to western Australia. This causes a shortage of rain and droughts in Africa.

17

Polar Dangers

Some of the most dangerous waters in the world for ships are the polar seas. In winter, the southern continent of Antarctica is a frozen sheet of solid ice. The Arctic, in the north, is covered for most of the year by thick floating ice. During an Arctic winter, fierce winds drive the ice together into jagged heaps.

Icebergs

A glacier is a huge, powerful river of ice that moves slowly down a mountainside. Glaciers produce many of the icebergs in the Arctic and Antarctica. When glaciers move down mountains and out to the sea, tides wear away into cracks in glaciers until large chunks of ice break off as icebergs. Once freed from the glacier, icebergs are pushed by currents into open waters until they eventually melt.

About 90 percent of an iceberg floats below the surface of the water. The destructive, unseen mass can tear and crush ships, causing them to sink. Foggy or misty weather can hide icebergs from view.

Floating ice

In winter, the Arctic and Antarctic oceans freeze in sheets called pack ice, which breaks up during the summer months. At this time, these waters provide a rich feeding ground for whales, seals, and walruses, which attracts fishers to the area. Polar temperatures never warm up enough for the ice to completely melt, and the floating ice eventually freezes back together in the winter.

Ships become stranded in floating ice as two or more large pieces of ice moving on currents crush into either side. Ships remain stuck until the following spring thaw.

Sea fog

Sea fog is also called **advection** fog, and it forms when warm moist air blows across cold ocean water. The air is cooled until it reaches its dew point, the point at which condensation occurs. The condensed water vapor creates a wall of mist that lowers visibility, or the distance sailors can see around the ship. Fifty years ago, helmsmen, or steering officers, relied on the sounds of foghorns and ships' bells to avoid collisions with passing ships in heavy fog. These crew members also kept watch for rocky coasts and icebergs. Today, modern ships use **radar** to help them navigate through sea fog.

(below) A tugboat pulls a damaged ship into a harbor in Sweden. In heavy fog, the passenger ship crashed into another ship, which tore a hole in the hull 36 feet (11 meters) long.

Disasters at Sea

There are countless shipwrecks lying on the bottom of the world's oceans. Some struck icebergs or oncoming boats, while others were lost in storms. Today, divers and treasure seekers venture into the chilly ocean waters to explore these wrecks.

Titanic

One of the most famous disasters at sea was the sinking of the passenger liner, Titanic, in 1912. That year, ice floes, pack ice, and icebergs had moved unusually far south, into the path of ships crossing the Atlantic Ocean. The Titanic struck an iceberg that cut a hole in the ship's hull 300 feet (91 meters) long. A distress call was sent out from the radio room aboard ship. The closest and fastest ship, Carpathia, took three and a half hours to reach the scene. By that time, 1,494 people had drowned. Only 712 people were saved.

Ice Patrol was established after the Titanic sunk in 1912. Using radar and planes, Ice Patrol monitors the path of ships and tries to keep them from colliding with icebergs. Ice Patrol warns boats over radio when they are dangerously close to floating ice.

Andrea Doria

In 1956, two passenger liners collided off the coast of New York in heavy fog. Crew members aboard the Andrea Doria detected the approach of the other ship, the Stockholm, on radar. The crew closed all watertight doors, posted lookouts, and sounded whistle warnings. As the Stockholm approached, it became clear that the ships' captains thought they were passing on either side but the ships ran headlong into each other. Out of the 1,706 people on board, 1,663 were rescued by the Stockholm and a nearby French liner.

1956

The Andrea Doria tips on its side before sinking 225 feet (69 meters) to the bottom of the Atlantic Ocean.

Capes

Some of the most dangerous sailing waters in the world are around the tip of South America, called Cape Horn, and the tip of South Africa, called the Cape of Good Hope. At least 800 ships have been lost off Cape Horn, where the Pacific and Atlantic oceans collide, causing waves more than 65 feet (20 meters) high. The Atlantic and Indian oceans meet in the Cape of Good Hope. The strong Agulhas current at the cape, combined with unstable winds, makes the waters dangerous to navigate through.

Karluk

In June 1913, a party of explorers set out from British Columbia, Canada, bound for the Arctic. Just two months after setting out, their ship, Karluk, became trapped in pack ice. Locked in ice, the ship drifted on ocean currents for five months before it was crushed and sunk. The crew got onto the pack ice while the captain, Robert Barlett set out to find help. The crew survived for one year, hunting Arctic animals for food. Rescue came in September 1914. Eleven crew members died from starvation and cold, thirteen survived.

1913

Forecasting

There are many warning systems, organizations, and scientists involved in forecasting weather conditions at sea. Oceanographers use various instruments to measure ocean currents, water temperature, and wave height. They also use Alvin, a deep-sea submarine, to monitor currents and other ocean phenomena in deep water.

Scientists use Alvin to track currents.

Measuring hurricanes

Meteorologists use planes, satellites, radar, and computers to track and rate hurricanes. Hurricanes are rated on a scale called the **Saffir-Simpson Scale**. A category one storm is weak, while a category five is the strongest storm. A category five storm is the rarest on the Saffir-Simpson Scale. The Sea, Lake, and Overland Surges from Hurricanes (SLOSH) is a computerized model used to predict the height of storm surge caused by hurricanes. Knowing potential wave height helps estimate how far inland the water might come. Coastal areas can be evacuated before a storm surge reaches land.

22-Sep   4:14

Satellite images of hurricanes help scientists see where and when the storms will hit land. In the Southern Hemisphere, hurricanes rotate in a clockwise direction. In the Northern Hemisphere, they spin counter-clockwise, or cyclonically.

Weather buoys

Automatic weather buoys are left in the ocean to transmit data to weather stations and passing satellites. The buoys carry various weather recording devices. Anemometers are instruments that measure windspeed. Barometers measure **air pressure**. Hygrometers measure the amount of moisture in the air. Scientists for the National Oceanic and Atmospheric Administration (NOAA) use ships to service and maintain the weather buoys. The NOAA has buoys in both the Atlantic and Pacific oceans. The information collected from buoys helps meteorologists predict all kinds of weather conditions.

This weather buoy monitors and transmits weather data in rough seas.

International Tsunami Warning System

Since 1948, an international organization has been working to warn coastal communities of approaching tsunamis. They do this to try to minimize the damage caused by the waves, and to allow people enough time to evacuate the region. Data on earthquakes and changes in sea levels are studied to figure out where a tsunami might strike and when. When scientists can see that a tsunami is about to strike, they send warning to local communities. Twenty-six countries in the Pacific belong to the International Tsunami Warning System.

Waves created by the wind are measured on a scale called the sea state. A zero sea state means the surface of the ocean is calm, while a nine sea state means waves are over 45 feet (14 meters) high.

Boat Safety

The Coast Guard is an organization that responds to people in trouble in the oceans. Many distress calls to Coast Guard stations come from small recreational crafts that have been trapped by an incoming tide, have experienced an accident, or caught on fire.

Stay on the boat!

Attempting to swim to shore is the worst thing you can do if you are stranded. Powerful currents can carry people even further out to sea, where they might drown. The biggest threat to a person who has been in the water is hypothermia. Hypothermia is a medical condition in which a person's body temperature falls below normal after being cold and wet. Hypothermia can kill a person in less than fifteen minutes if the water temperature is less than 32° Fahrenheit (0° Celsius). Rescuers wrap hypothermia victims in blankets to try to raise their body temperatures back to normal.

Radio for help!

One of the easiest ways to ensure safety at sea is to carry a radio to make a distress call if necessary. Distress is when a boat is in a situation where passengers are in danger. Special channels on VHF FM (Very High Frequency) radio are used for specific purposes. Channel 13 is used by ships to communicate with each other. The Coast Guard regularly issues weather updates and warnings to boats at sea using VHF FM.

Channel 16 is monitored continually by the Coast Guard and used only for distress calls. When a distress call comes in, the Coast Guard sends a rescue boat or an aircraft to help the victims.

Before you go

There are a number of items you should bring boating, even if you plan to be gone for only a few hours.

1. Pack a watertight bag that contains sunscreen, hat, sunglasses, rain gear, and a first aid kit.
2. Check the boat. Make sure the fuel tanks are full, the engine is properly tuned and there are no fuel leaks.
3. Check safety equipment. The operator of the boat should have completed a nationally recognized boating course. The operator should also have a compass and navigation charts. Everyone onboard should wear a lifejacket or a Personal Floatation Device (PFD) that fits properly.
4. Bring a radio. At the very least, bring along an AM radio to get weather reports.

5. Make sure to have a flashlight, fire extinguisher, paddle, and a bailer onboard.
6. Be sure the boat is equipped with an anchor and line to keep from drifting further out to sea if stranded.

Signal flares alert rescuers to a boat's position.

How to make a distress call

1. MAYDAY 3 times
2. This is (name of boat 3 times)
3. Repeat Mayday and name of boat
4. Give position
5. Nature of emergency
6. Kind of assistance required
7. Number of people onboard and any problems, such as injuries
8. Description of boat

The main cause of boat fires is leaking fuel and fuel vapors.

 FIRST AID KIT
PREMIERS SOINS

Rescue at Sea

Large ships risk greater danger during ocean storms because they go further out to sea, often beyond the range of Coast Guard stations. If the ship cannot ride out the storm, another ship may be close enough to answer a distress call and come to the ship's rescue.

A helicopter lowers a rescuer on a winch into the water to save a victim. The victim will be brought to the hospital to receive treatment for injuries.

AMVER

AMVER is short for Automated Mutual Assistance Vessel Rescue System. AMVER is available to ships all over the world. Sailors can regularly report the ship's position to a computer database in Martinsburg, West Virginia. If a Coast Guard station receives a distress call from a ship way out to sea, they check for ships nearby and send them to help the ship that is in distress.

Air rescue

Helicopters and lifeboats often coordinate their efforts to rescue ships at sea. Helicopters can reach places that are far out to sea much faster than boats can. Helicopters can also speed injured passengers to the hospital for medical attention. To get an injured person into the helicopter, a rescuer on a winch is lowered from the helicopter. The victim is then strapped securely into a basket stretcher. The rescuer uses radio and hand signals to communicate with the helicopter operators. Both victim and rescuer are raised up to the helicopter.

Lighthouses

Lighthouses are built on coasts or offshore rocks to warn sailors of dangers in the water and to help guide them safely into harbors. They use both light and sound to warn ships of fog. The sound of a foghorn can be heard for about 20 miles (30 km) over water. In the past, lighthouses were run by lighthouse keepers who lit the lamp at dusk, put it out at dawn, cleaned the lenses, operated the foghorn, and even tried to rescue sailors! Today, lighthouses operate automatically. In some places, lightships and automatic navigational buoys do the work that lighthouses once did. Radar on ships also helps boats to navigate in darkness and fog.

Life rafts and lifeboats

Modern life rafts are dome-shaped canopies on inflatable tubes, that are specially designed to stay afloat in rough seas. The overhead canopy protects people from the sun and cold. Survival packs with food and fresh water help victims survive on the raft while waiting for help. Most ships are equipped with several life rafts. Lifeboats are speedy, unsinkable boats used by the Coast Guard. These boats are equipped with automatic navigation systems that help rescuers locate a boat in distress.

Rotating lenses surround lights in a lighthouse. A motor moves the lenses so that the light scans across the water.

People board a lifeboat after violent seas destroyed their boat.

After the Storm

Storms that move inland to strike coastal communities can cause costly damage to property, lives, and the environment. Proper preparation before a storm hits can help to lower these costs.

Land damage

The strong winds caused by hurricanes can uproot trees, knock over buildings, tip cars and trucks, and send objects hurtling through the air. Winds can knock out power lines and leave communities without electricity for days or weeks. Flooding is another result of hurricanes hitting land. The amount of rain that falls during a hurricane can wash out roads and cause riverbanks to break. In some places, flooding can cause landslides and mudslides, which speed down hillsides, destroying everything in their paths. Storm surges caused by winds during hurricanes cause the sea level to rise along coasts. Homes and businesses can be flooded by storm surges and people trapped in buildings may drown.

On July 17, 1998 a tsunami hit the Saundaun province of Papua New Guinea, wiping out two seaside villages and destroying most of two others. About 3,000 people

Bulldozers form protective flood barriers by pushing sand up the beach. The artificial sand dunes will prevent rising sea levels from destroying homes and perhaps even save lives.

Cleaning up

After a storm, relief organizations come into an area to help the survivors rebuild their communities. Some organizations, such as the Federal Emergency Management Agency (FEMA) in the United States, are government organizations that work with local and state governments to clean up after a disaster. International organizations, such as the Red Cross, work with local governments to repair buildings, provide medical service, and raise money to buy food, clothing, and shelter for victims. Individuals can also help by volunteering their time, money, and other supplies to help the survivors of a disaster.

Community preparedness

Coastal communities around the world do their best to try to protect themselves from ocean storms. One way of protecting the coasts from storm waves is to build seawalls and flood barriers. A seawall is a tall wall, usually made of concrete and metal. Seawalls are constructed in areas that are especially vulnerable to damage from ocean storms.

Over time, heavy surf wears away at buildings and other infrastructure.

Recipe for Disaster

Huge, heavy ocean tankers and small recreational crafts all float on the surface of the ocean. Try this experiment to find out why boats float, and why they sink!

What you need:

* A plastic garbage bag to cover the work surface
* Modeling clay
* A large deep bowl filled three-quarters full with water
* Several pennies

What to do:

1. Shape modeling clay into a solid, round ball. Put the ball in the water. What happens?

2. Remove the clay ball from water. Shape the clay into a boat by flattening it and turning up the sides.

3. Put the boat carefully into the water. Now what happens?

4. Add pennies one at a time to your floating boat. How many pennies does it take to sink your boat?

What you will see:

Boats float because of buoyancy. Buoyancy is the upward force of water that presses against objects placed in it. The ball in your experiment sank while the boat floated because the boat was flatter, allowing more water to push against it than the ball. When you added pennies to your boat, you increased the weight of the boat until the force of the boat pushing down on the water was stronger than the buoyancy. This is what happens when boats take on too much water in ocean storms. Rescue your boat and try the experiment over, only this time create a whirlpool by swirling your finger in the water. Can your boat ride out the "storm"?

Glossary

advection A change in temperature in an air mass as it moves from one place to another

air pressure The force of air against other objects

climate Weather that occurs in a particular region

condense To change from a gas to a liquid

convection Heat transfer in a gas or liquid

deflect To cause to turn aside or bend

density The measure of how closely packed the parts of an object are

displaced When something is moved or shifted from its usual position

evaporate To change from a liquid to a gas

fjord A long, deep ocean inlet between mountains

friction Rubbing action between two things

heat energy The energy given off by the sun or another heat source

ice floe A large, floating mass of ice

infrastructure The basic services needed by a community, such as bridges and power lines

meteorologists Scientists who study weather

nutrients Parts of food that plants and animals need in order to stay healthy

oceanographer A scientist who studies oceans

plankton Very small plants and animals that float in water

radar A device that uses the echo of radio waves to determine the location of an object

Saffir-Simpson Scale A scale used to indicate the severity of hurricanes

salinity The amount of salt in water

satellite A body that orbits the Earth and takes pictures of the clouds to help scientists forecast

tectonic plates Large, rocky plates that make up the Earth's crust, or outermost layer

Index